Terry's Travels

Terry's Travels

MY LIFE IN WORDS & PICTURES

Terry Boothby

To order additional copies of this book, contact:
Xlibris
800-056-3182
www.Xlibrispublishing.co.uk
Orders@Xlibrispublishing.co.uk
663810

Foreword

The author was born in a small town in North Yorkshire in the January of 1934. His grandfather had a large family – 7 girls and 3 boys.

All their names were from the bible – Ethel, Mary, Eve, Ann, Rose, Lilian and Edith, the boys were named Jess, David & James.

So when it came to the authors christening his parents had decided on his name but grandfather wanted him to also have a name from the bible. The youngest boy James was given the task of going through the bible and giving his views of what he had found. Grandfather said "The name must not be an everday name that can be shortened or used as a nickname. James took 2 days before he suggested his answer, and knowing his father would not like the name chosen so James told Jess his older brother that there were only 2 names that were not used often and they could not be used – "Jesus and God" so Jess made a decision that 'Lord' was the answer. I have for many years, after talking to lots of people, taken heed of a remark repeated many times by my listeners (including my wife). It was suggested I should write a book of short stories of my adventures (trials and tribulations) of my career.

I left my grammar school in 1950 not with many academic results – but top notch at every sporting event – except cricket.

I trained (5 mile run) every evening hoping that I could achieve "Victor Ludorum" like my cousin Keith did in 1948. So I had a challenge as well as a mixed home life to contend with.

My father left home when I was 10 years old, so I had no assitance with any of my school work. My mother had been 'in service' from when she left school till she got married at the age of 25. So, she could teach me how to set a top table and which glasses should be used etc.

So I started work at Dorman Long Steelworks at Carlin How (Yorks) or Skinnin Grove which was 2 miles from home; I worked in the Rolling Mill – rolling all shapes of steel. I started on the 'finishing' part of the mill, within 2 months I was promoted to the 'roughing' side of the mill operation this side paid a little more and involved moving the main rollers up & down to shape the steel (working in fractions). My next promotion was 4 months later I was to help with the roll changes and then "cogging" – this was rolling and tipping 15 ton ingots of hot steel straight from the ovens – I thought it was easier than my 2 previous jobs as I did not have to operate rollers and I did not have to move the large (main) rollers up & down. It was a 3 man position

So I had this job at about £4 a week, working 6am-2pm, 2pm-10pm, 10pm-6am, and when there was a change of steel to be rolled (6" x 2" joust to railway lines) we had about 2 hours waiting time – so I worked with my uncle (on the overhead crane) & qualified to operate singly. So altogether I could earn £6½ a week

At this time my sister–(younger by 18 months) had a job as a shop assistant my mother worked full-time in a dry cleaners. Shop and every evening as an usherette in the local cinema and so life went on.

I was disappointed in myself as all the other boys I went to school with were at Cambridge University or working in banks 3 or 4 were naval officers, 2 were in customs and exise. So I packed in the job at Skinningrove (Feb 1952) as I knew national service was due as I 18.

I sat and talked it out with my sister as my mother had enough on her plate keeping us.

My sister was very academic (night school 4 nights a week) so I took a part-time job – delivering-movietone news from cinema to cinema 1st & 2nd shows for this I was paid 6 shilling a week / which I gave to my sister – to pay her bus fares to night school (40 singl & 6d return) so it subsidised her

My sister told me that if I joined for 2 years – it was not long enough to learn a trade so we talked it out with friends and I met a boy in the Raf who was on leave from southen Rhodesia, after talking to him it opened a new door to my life he was an airframe mechaic and he said it was a good life.

So my sister suggested I should go for longer and maybe I would get a trade and maybe travel.

I had not seen my father for 7 years so I had no ties there we explained to my mother I would be away for a long time but would send money home (7 shilings a week)

So I went for my interview/I must at this point tell you I took and passed my city & guild in iron and steel so I did achieve a litle at Dorman Long. My 3 uncles & my grandfather all worked at Skinningrove till they reached retirement age.

I signed up in the Raf for 3 years and was told I would go on course –Airframe mechani???

I went to Raf West Kirby near Liverpool for my "square bashing". I enjoyed the physical effort required and improved my dancing – having danced since 5 year old (ballroom) my mother & father had medals for dancing I also have 2 uncles who are dance instructors.

After West Kirby I was posted on my Airframe course at St Athan (S Wales) it was quite an adventure I had never gone further than 30 miles from home before.

I was at St Athan for 6 months and passed out as an Airframe Mechanic. But the bonus was I met many interesting people as every week there was a big dance – in the gymnasium so I attended every week – I met a girl called Elsie Scrine – a good dancer who lived in Swansea. – at that time her elder brother played football for Swansea & Wales.

1 night she invited myself and 3 more airmen to her house in Swansea we accepted. And went to Swansea for 2 days – it was marvellous. We walked all over Swansea incuding "the mumbles" see Swansea history

After my 6 months at St Athan I was posted to Raf Duxford (Cambridge). I teamed up with another mechanic called Ron Reece – we went out to Cambridge normally on a Sunday evening. We travelled by bus about 6pm and caught the 930 pm bus back to Duxford. One Sunday evening a young lady was sat at the rear of the bus crying her eyes out. She had twisted her leg and the knee had dislocated. So after chatting for a while Ron suggested she should try to sleep – he also said I should sit next to the window and she could rest on my shoulder. This was in 1953 – I married that girl in 1955 and next year is our diamond wedding (60 years).

After returning to Duxford (taking the young lady to sick quarters) the next day I was woken up at 430 am and told to get dressed also to wear my kerosene overalls over my normal wear. We were given rubber boots. The overalls were some kind of polypropolene – at 630 am we boarded a coach and after a 2½ hr journey we were briefed that we were on flood relief in Se of Essex – we were left in a church hall and given a sleeping bag each then we had a meal from a field kitchen and each of us was given a pint pot.

The next day we wer taken to where the water had broken through the dykes and commenced filling sandbags we worked till 7pm and were taken back to Southminster Church Hall – by this time we had all been given a fold up camp bed each. So at last we had a decent nights sleep that night.

We worked for 7 days on flood relief and then we were replaced by other servicemen including some Americans and so life went on and I was able to meet the young lady who was now working as a telephonist at Duxford. PBX.

I served my 3 years in the Raf and I married in 1955 (Feb) demobbed in April and searched for accomodation in the Northampton area. We were lucky as we both got a job on 72 Mu (maintenance) working for the Raf.

After working at the Mu for 9 months we heard of the services wage structure being altered. So my old 37 shillings was increased to £6. So we worked out that we would be better off if I rejoined the Raf and we would (in time) get accomodation in a married quarter. After reviewing all the pro's and cons we decided that life would be better if I rejoined the Raf. In October 1956 I signed for 3 years in the Raf.

We were posted to Bassingbourn (Cambs) Nr Royston. I settled in fairly quickly and enjoyed my work and my wife was employed (telephonist) on the Raf PBX, plus we were allocated a 2 bedroom house on the base. So everything seem to be hunky-dory in 1958 I was sent to Raf Weeton Nr Blackpool on an Airframe fitters course. After 6 months I was qualified and promoted to junior technician and then returned to Bassingbourn. 3 months later we were posted to Germany (and so we had our 1st taste of overseas) – my wife came to Germany to join me after 10 months of separation. I must say we both thoroughly enjoyed our time in Germany. We bought our 1st car a VW Beetle and travelled the breadth and width of West Germany

When our tour in Germany finished, I had a new posting to Raf Abingdon (Berks). I was promoted to corporal and we had a lovely married quarter house. My wife had been to see why she was having problems getting pregnant and was informed that there maybe some problems. We had been married 7 years and so wanted a child. So in 1962 I worked on Beverley A/C Hasting A/C and all station flight A/C.

In 1963 a girl-friend of my wife (both ex-Raf) informed us she had met a girl who was pregnant (but unmarried) and she did not want to keep the baby. She intended putting the child up for adoption. My wife was so pleased (we adopted a 7 day old baby girl) and our life was now completed. – I had signed on during this time till my 55th year

In 1964 I volunteered to become aircrew (loadmaster), I was accepted and went on a 1 year course (for flight engineer) – there appeared to be a shortage of Flt Engineers and too many volunteers for Airloadmasters. There was ony a difference in pay of 6d a day so off I went on my course. It was a good course and I enjoyed being taught electrics and instroments. I passed the course and went to Bigginhill to await posting.

My wife was still at Raf Abingdon so when I discussed my position with the selection board at Biggin-Hill – they decided to send me on an outward bound course. Hiking in Scotland and then rowing down Lochness – after telling the board what I intended to do after their course was a parachute course – at Abingdon as my wife was at Abingdon – they agreed and sent me straight from the course at Abingdon to Thorney-Island on a Airloadmaster course. I passed both the courses and was posted to Raf Colerne on 24 Sqdn Hastings A/C. so I had my first taste of the Middle East, Aden, Salalah, Sharjah, Dubai, Bahrein, my squadron covered all these airfields and we had parachute drops at most airfields. Having now being qualified as Flt Engineer and airloadmaster the Raf posted me to Raf Abingdon on 46 sqn (they do not have Flt Engineers on Andover (748) A/C so I was a Air Quartermaster. Looking back over my Raf time it was probably the best move they ever made.

On 46 sqd I was posted on a 14 month detachment at Sharjah (the experience I had from this posting was excellent,

I travelled to Islamabad – Tehran Thessalonika, Calcutta- Cyprus nearly all on 1 week exercises

My last 3 months of my 14 month tour I was posted to Bahrein on a VIP flight it was on this posting I managed to equip myself and have all my KD uniforms made in Singapore (as the Air Commodre suggested) I have since been back to Singapor and Av Wai Lam (the tailor) still has my sizes in his order book (40 years have elapsed since my 1st order

So ended my tour in the Middle East and back to Raf Abingdon.– By now it was 1969 so 1970 the Sqdn (46) moved to Raf Thorney Island – my first exercise from there was named Bersatu-Pardu. So we flew to Singapore and then Kuala-Lumpur. For a 7 week exercise (flying every day with 1 A/C and 2 crews.

It was then a card from my wife informed me she was pregnant. So after 16 years she succeeded in having a child (1971)

In August 1971 she had a baby girl but not without problems. The baby had hydrcepalous problems and had a valve put into her head but now at the age of 41 she is OK now

1973 – I left 46 sqn for 99 sqn (Brize-Norton Brittania A/C. from Brize Norton we had lots of flights to America, Canada, Belize and the evacuation of Cyprus.

After 3 years of travelling the world I decided to take the golden handshake as it was called, I was by this time the rank of master aircrew (w/o)

We bought a house in Carterton and settled down (for a while). I picked up a "flight" magazine and saw a job advertised that would suit me. I went to Crawley (Sussex) for an interview and lo and behold in the waiting room were 6 men who I had known for at least 10 years. So I was accepted at the interview and was employed by Redcoat Air Cargo – they had 3 Brittania A/C which carried cargo to West Africa – Accra and Lagos and the occasional contract for mod sometimes to Cyprus or Belize.

Most of the work was in West Africa – refuel in Spain – then Banjol – Freetown, Abijan & then Accra, the return leg was Freetown, Banjul then was Palmas or Tenerife. We picked up tomatoes for Marks & Spencer. One trip stands out from most of the others I received a phone call on Sunday afternoon "Would I report to Luton" as quick as possible. I arrived at Luton the A/C was empty and we then flew to Belgium the capt was upset as it had ruined his golf game on a Sunday – he didnt seem to trust Redcoat but as long as he had some work he was happy. In Belgium they marshalled the A/C into a hangar miles from the runway. The load was 9 ton of bang (explosives) which meant we all increased our hourly rate by £5 per hr. We flew back to Luton and customs appered they seemed to know all about the load. They informed us we had to park on a certain parking pan and the load must be guarded. They sealed the doors (which were also locked) an I put down my bunk for the night I went through the manifests for the load and made a mental note what I had to inform the A/C Capt of the next day. Before we left Luton 500 kgs of cargo were loaded to go to Banjul this meant that people in Banjul would see our A/C load so I had to alter the load so that none of the bang would be seen and the offload was from the belly-hold and A/C doors were kept closed and locked

While tidying up the chains & cargo nets I thought back to the manifests "The Rod and Gun Club" – Fretown this smelt fishy to me so I uncovered part of 1 pallet and read from th ammunition box – 3 ball – 1 tracer so that settled it – I informed the capt who was even more upset as Luton ops had kept info to themselves. The capt there and then infod Luton on dadio tht instead of £5 per hr, he would pay the crew £10 per hour – there was no objection from Luton

A smilar trip took place later in the same year. Late on a Sunday evening we flew to Belgium – loaded the A/C the load was palletised and covered up. The paperwork just declared H/E (High Explosive) and was addressed to a particular – colonel. He would meet us when we landed. Everything went to plan and I was informed we would load 97 chest – of tea foila return load.

When we landed we taxied quite a way and then '2 lage fork lifts stood waiting to offload our A/C. It took about 45 minutes to off load, the pallets were taken inside a hangar and placed just inside the door I noticed as the last pallet went into the hangar the doors at the other end of the hangar opened and a C130 A/C was parked there

I quickly ran into the hangar to the C1310 (Hercules) and spoke to the airloadmaster (who didnt know too much) but then I spoke to the navigator who told me they were delivering land mines to the border of Namimbia.

I told my capt what our load had been, so he again informed Luton ops that he would be paying £10 per hr dangerous cargo money again ops did not object at all.

Joining the common market. This is a day I will always remember. I was going to Banjul with drilling equipment. Luton ops had informed me that I had a return load of mangoes they did not know how many. But we got paid by the kilo so it did not matter

I offloaded the A/C in about 2 hours. We organised a loading team to load the man goes. The load was in hessian sacks – it was then that I realised I needed trip trays and some large plastic sheeting to protect A/C floor the hessian were place in the drip trays. The manifest said 7300 kgs I thought that the load I had was not that weight so I check weighed 10 sacks – the load was underweight by 1300 kgs.

So I altered the manifest to show the correct wt. I also had to do a new trim sheet. I informed the captain of the difference in wt of the cargo (he informed Luton ops) that the manifest had been altered to show correct wt of cargo and so we set off for Luton.

We arrived at Luton about 1 pm the customs came on board and took their copies of all the paperwork. I went to my firms office and explained to my managing director about the changes; I had made.

Within 5 minutes customs phoned me and said they wanted to see me. I went to their office and explained the situation and was shocked to learn that customs were fining me £150. After listening to them briefing me on common market rules & showing me the new European manifests which could not be altered – a new manifest should have been raised. I explained that Banjul did not have the new manifests yet so they used the pre-common market paperwork

But to no avail I paid the £150 and explained – my office also did not have any new European manifests. So I remember that first day of the UK joining the common market – through my empty wallet.

As things worked out it was not too bad a day. My boss gave me £150 and said "Forget all about it" and the importer came to the office the next day and gave me £50 (As the price of the fruit was a "shortage in which case he sold it at a better price so ended my 1st day of common market rules

One of my most memorable trips was in 1970 I was stationed at 'Thorney Island' (Hampshire) I was detailed to go on exercise "Bersatu-Pardu" at Kuala-Lumpur the trip outbound (with 28 of our own groundcrew) was via 'Istres' (France) to Malta and then Cyprus. Then the 2nd day to Tehran and on to Sharjah (Oman) 2 days rest and then to Calcutta then to Gan and onto Bangkok and after 10 hours rest onto Singapore – 2 day rest and then to Kuala-Lumpur

The exercise was mainly passenger carrying to the east side of the country so that their forces were operating correctly. So our passengers included the "King for a year" and ranks of colonels and above (VIPs). As we ony had one A/C I flew every 2 days while another airloadmaster flew alternate days.

While I was at Kuala-Lumpur I contacted a virus also 16 of my ground crew, we were flown to Changi Hospital (Singapore)

After 6 days in hospital we all went back to Kuala-Lumpur where I had a letter & card from my wife. The cards picture was an old man and old lady – she said "Ill give it to you just one more time for luck" it informed me my wife was pregnant with our first child

We were in our 16th year of marriage so I had a little drink that night to celebrate. So far our part on the exercise was not perfect – with ½ our team in hospital so on our return to Kuala-Lumpur the co-pilot left the imprest in Singapore (which proved he had spent too long being ADC to royalty and not enough time learning about supporting your squadron personnel. It worked well as the imprest was sent to us 2 days later.

The detachment went well for 4 weeks and then we planned to return to UK. Via Bangkok-Bombay then Sharjah (where we had a sister squadron (84) of Andover A/C (748). We had been fully serviceable for 6 weeks but on the Bombay-Sharjah leg we lost total hydraulic power. So after pumping the undercarridge system down. Luckily Sharjah had Andover mechanics posted there so they knew how to handle the A/C. They took it into the hangar lifted it on jacks and tested the hydraulic system and found 2 pin size holes in 2 hydraulic pipes in the nose undercarriage. We sent signals to Thorney Island and Abingdon for spare parts. We were advised to carry 30 litres of hydraulic oil if we went any decent distances (especially over the desert) so we loaded our A/C with 20 gallon of water and 40 litres of hydraulic oil. (The captain said having weight down the tail helped to keep us in trim better.

So we went to Tehran and ran out of hydraulics while on their runway – we were towed off the runway and we filled the oil system to allow us to fly to Sharjah. When we arrived in Sharjah our A/C spares had been delivered so after fitting the new pipes we could continue flying to UK (via Cyprus & Istres) all in all the whole exercise seemed to be uncomfortable (not of a good standard)

While flying for Redcoat Air Cargo (late 1970s I used to go to Accra every Monday and Thursday so the offload teams in Accra knew our crew quite well. The majority of the loaders were aged 20-30 years old. So to encourage them to offloads & load quite quickly I thought up a system to reward them (not all at once) so when we landed in Accra – I changed out of uniform into a colourful T shirt & jeans. I could tell from their chatter they admired the T shirt (Bright yellow with a red racing car as the pattern) so I told them that the man that worked the hardest and quickest would receive the T-shirt. They system seem to work so I had 2 new (and different) T shirts each week. One of the things the loaders did was to chew cocoa beans so the caffeine worked to keep them happy. Once a month I arranged for them to bring me some pineapples – they did 20 items which they asked for £5 English money it was such a good deal.

In the early (1967) November I went on an exercise at El-Adem (Libya) we were flying Hastings A/C. We took 4 A/C and we practised supply dropping daily. On the outbound leg to El-Adem one of our A/C picked up some items for delivery to the group captain O/C of El-Adem

We had been there 4 days when someone enquired about the items for the C/O. One of another crew admitted he had forgotten the items and they were still in the belly hold of his A/C. Well after 4 days of temperature of 45°. I believe the items had all melted. It turned out they had been a birthday cake and a Christmas cake for the group captain. How that airman explained that mistake I'll never know – but he never talked about it.

In 1978 I received a phone call from Luton operations – would I report as quickly as possible to load and deliver some furniture

I drove to Luton and was told that 3 removel lorries had my load for my A/C I was also given some notes regarding the freight to be loaded.

When I saw the furniture, each item had a note on it, it was then I realised the cost of this furniture was enormous. It was all copied from well known pieces.

Copies of Chippendale and other famous furniture makers. Each item had the position it should occupy in the house and even the bedrooms I phoned the shipping agent and enquired about the load after estimating the weight of the freight that would be carried. The shipping agent asked me why I was querying the load. I replied telling him that he did not know who was delivering the furnture – he seemed to think that as we flew the load in that we were responsible to deliver the furnture. I informed him that we would only on the ground for 2 hrs – he then replied – how much would the whole job cost. I said I have no idea, that would be decided by my firms operations. He then spoke to our firm and they were told that money was no object. My ops said to me "Its a very good contract" they finally agreed that it would be £28000, to fly the load and if they were satisfied that nothing was scratched or broken they would pay £5000 more. So it was agreed. I didnt even ask if there was a return load. We loaded the furniture making sure it was not scratched or bumped at all, we wrapped blankets round everything. The attached labels told us where all the furniture should be positioned such as "Prince Amias bedroom (pink walls) 2 foot from window ledge & 2 foot from the wardrobe. The hardest part was <u>briefing</u> the ten men we paid to offload and load the removal vans that were waiting for us.

To cut the story short, it took 3 hrs to offload the A/C and 45 mins to drive to the destination house. – It was the largest house I have ever seen – there were 25 rooms and huge steel gates at the bottom of the drive. The position of this house was on an island just 4 mile from the West African coast south of Abijdon. Watching the handling of the furniture – seemed so slow and keeping an eye on each item as they were positioned 1 by 1. It was 9 oclock in the evening when finish moving all the furniture. I went the local hotel who expected us and made us welcome with 2 bottles of whisky – some sandwiches and 5 room keys. When I said hotel it was an African Hotel not 3 star or even 1 star. No air conditioning some rooms had no glass in the windows but as it was explained "You are on the 4th floor –" no one can get in the window" 2 clean sheets laid on the bed which was not made up.

At 10 am the next day we went to our A/craft and a gentleman spoke to us and gave us a letter.

It would appear he was related to a very rich family of Arabs (who were in the oil business) and he informed us his relatives had asked if we could take a similar load to Riyaadh in 14 days time. He said he thought our firm gave value for money. So our firm did some valuable business with an Arabian prince who didn't care how much money we charged. I did ask one question "Could the labels on the furniture be written in Arabic. (Next time)

My next managment job was in Toronto Airport – the cargo manager was going on 6 weeks holiday – would I replace him. As we had just been operating at that airport my firm agreed they would send me.

I arrived and was told I had 15 Italians to work for me. I found 1 Italian spoke a little German so we decided he was my spokesman.

We had at that time problems in the car factory in Saarbruken (Germany) if the production line shut down it would cost in the bill nearly one million dollars to restart the line. So our job was to keep Saarbrucken supplied with car parts. We had to offload 3 large vehicles loaded with back axles of different type vehicles and if there was more room on the A/C (belly holds) any other car parts could be sent. So we sent 3 A/C every day 8 hrs between them. My first idea was to make the offloading of the lorries easier so I made sure they parked 200 metres nearer our hangar. Then with the help of my German speaking Italian – we ordered 2 "Gabestapler" or forklifts in English. Just doing the job shortened the loading time by 1 hr 45 mins.

We carried on this job for 3 weeks till we found at that because of bad weather in Germany (2 foot of snow) they had problems keeping up with us and had a backlog of axles

So my firm decided (as I spoke German) I should go to Dusseldorf Airport and sort out their problems. Soon I was on my way, at Dusseldor I booked a hotel as close as I could to the cargo terminal, it was 6 miles travel to go to the airport. This was caused because there was no way to cross the autoban. So a taxi took me to work at 1 am & return at 9 am, then another taxi a 4pm & return at 11pm. Soon I realised it was very expensive paying for all these taxis. So the manager of the hotel told me to go and talk with the hotel gardener. I did and he revealed at the bottom of the garden there was a tunnel underneath autobahn so from then onwards I borrowed his bycycle & the distance was about 2 miles to the cargo terminal this saved me paying all taxi fares about 300 marks a day.

My company did not mind as long as I was there to meet the 3 AC per day & off load them, they would pay the taxi fares

We soon had it working like clockwork??? The money saved on taxis paid the A/C landing fees and take/off fees. As I had no licence to take large amounts of money out of the country, I used to provide 1 bottle & 200 cigs to each member of each A/C, for which they paid for in German marks. After claiming so much of my wages I had enough to pay the landing and tak/off fees. Keeping my eye on the exchange rate I was able to make quite a little profit especially as the airport said I could pay fees once a month (Instead of daily. So each crew that came in had a hot meal, 1 bottle & 200 cigs each. They were very pleased. The taxi I had to Saarbrucken cost 350 mds so I only went twice in my detachment but it was quite a profitable detachment (although I spent a longtime at the airport, working and slept the rest of the time in the hotel.

Sometimes life can be quite exiting even acidentaly dangerous. This happened while I was on a trip to Belize, we took a taxi from the airport to Belize City – the weather was atrocius-torrential. Rain and strong winds. The taxi driver (Otis) was our regular driver and we all thought he was a careful driver

But that day we had second thoughts I had never heard of "Aqua-Planing" but that day we experienced it – we left the road and finished near the river (6 foot) the road was at least 30 yards behind us. It was frightening I though my life was ending it was only pure luck that the car stopped 6 foot from the wide river.

One summer day I had just arrived in Bermuda (We were shuttling troops from Belize to Bermuda and as we were the only Raf A/C with a tail wheel which allowed us to land at Belize. It took 2 more yers before they lenghed the runway and cut down thousand of trees at the ends of the runway and also either side of the runway. Anway I was walking to get a taxi to the hotel it was only when I reached the hotel and went to pay for the taxi that I realised someone had taken my wallet from my pocket – it was then when I remember someone bumping into me at the airport. He had my wallet but I had my passport, driving licence & credit card in my briefcase. So I could still pay my bills. I now have a zip and velcro on my inside pocket

I sometimes sit and think – have I been lucky during my life or have I had friends who were lucky. The following story might explain what I call "luck" I was still posted to Sharjah (Oman)

I was chosen to go on an exercise in Greece. We flew via – Tehran and Thessalonika. Our detachment was 2 A/C and 20 groundcrew (84 sqdn personnel). On the exercise, the following nationalities were involved, American, German English and Greeks. The Americans brought a huge mobile laundry with them, the English had to provide all member nations with food from a field kitchen unit. Luckily for me, the warrant officer (English) who had command of the field kitchen was the brother-in-law of 1 of my airloadmasters, which sorted any problems regarding eating for the next 4 weeks.

Our mission on this exercise was to air-drop supplies to the different groups of soldiers about 40 miles from the main base. The exercise worked very well for 3 weeks. But one day the A/C loaders went haywire sending field food (compo rations all tinned) they sent the German load to the Greeks – the Ameircan food to the English and the German food to the Americans so you can imagine the results.

As ther was no washing facilities where we were camping we had to use our "scouting instincts" and provide our own solution

We found 1 water tap (cold water) in an old toilet next to the A/C dispersal we bought 50 foot of hose and some copper tubing and 3 showerheads (roses or spouts). We fixed it all up in some trees by a high wall and showered daily at 730am for 30 mins. There were complaints from the office staff on the opposite side of the A/C dispersal – too many naked men every morning – so we went out a bought plastic sheeting so that the shower area was competely covered. The Americans could use the shower at set times 8-830am. If they provided the English cook with eggs &

sausages daily. So the exercise went well, the Greek & Germans supplied fresh vegetables and meat too our English cooks. The Americans did not charge to use their laundry. – So everyone was happy.

My last detachenent in the Raf was in 1976. I was to take 30 men to Bardufoss (Norway). I was to be "Segeant Major" of Aialce whatever that meant. My C/O was a Canadian colonel. The exercise was for A/C to bring men to Bardufoss and support them for 4 weeks. I had a meeting with the colonel and asked "What are my terms of refence; he replied by giving me a cigar and telling me that my job was to stop people coming to his office and complaining about anything = that meant I had a free hand regarding – accomodation, transport, feeding the different nations, and off-loading and on loading all types of A/C involved on the exercise. His afterthought was don't forget the Americans expect every empty coca cola tin to be returned on their A/C – 2 cents a can.

This turned out to be nearly 30% of the exercise. Ive had 6 A/C competely full of coca-cola cans. Fuly palletised and each A/C was full.

So afte arranging 2 barrack blocks for the support staff and visiting aircrew. I then had a discussion with the head Raf cook who suggested that because of the low temperatures he would only serve hot meals provided he had the money to buy the meat and vegetables.

So we decided that $10 would provde 3 meals per person per day. The first large problem was feeding – every day crews from Germany-Italy UK- and America so the kitchens were only closed from 3am-5am daily – luckily we had enough UK cooks to manage those hours. The Canadians had sent barmen-stewards and some drivers for the exercise. All the offloading transport – condecs, forklifts, tractors and trolleys were handled by the Canadians

The charge for eating – after making a roll call list of personnel seem to work ok then some American A/C came in with 3 crews per A/C they had flown from the west of America & used 3 crew arriving in Norway. The A/C captain paid $240 for his crews which only stayed 10 hrs at Bardufoss. So. So after 1 week I had so much American money that I signalled Raf Lyneaam to send a financial officer from pay accounts to Bardufoss

He arrived the next day and I had 2 bulging safes for him to work with. He stated by giving money back to the officer in charge of each nation – American-Canadian-German-Italian. But after he had departed the money still kept rolling in. The Canadians barmen had never seen such money, every A/C member who arrived bought a bottle of spirits – 200 cigarettes or cigars back with them I took dollars from my 2 safes to the local bank and had a chat with the manager about exchange rates. It appered the Norwegian exchange seemed to alter daily as did the dollar against the pound. Th German money stayed still I ended up with a bank account of Norwegian Kroner. This went on another weeks the value of the kroner fell so I changed all the money to pounds. This made it possible for me to provide a bottle and 200 for the crews who visited us.

The colonel (IC) suggested we should have some R & R. As the exercise slowed over the weekend (No Al on Saturday or Sunday) I think it must have an Emerican holiday weekend.

So I made a phone call to hire-car company and they suggested a route where my colonel could see the Fjords and go inside 60° north. I talked to him about this and he agreed I could hire 2 Mercedes cars so that he plus 2 other officer would drive one and his adjutant + 2 more officers could use the othe car gave him the suggested rout and pointed out the tyres had snow tyres on each car

Then I phoned to British Embassy in Oslo and asked to speak to a member of the VIP Andover Crew. I spoke to the co-pilot & the navigator and they said they had not done any continuation flying for over 1 month. I knew that this type of flying must be done at least once a month

So with their captains views being considered they agreed that they could fly to Bardufoss on Friday afternoon and then upto the artic circle where they would land & drop off 40 airmen and fly to Oslo. Then on Monday morning fly to the airport inside 60° north pick-up the 40 pax & take them back to Bardufoss. I will at this pont mention that I had flown with the pilot an co-pilot earlier in my career in El-Adem and other bases in the Middle-East. So we were quite good friends

So Friday morning came and I had to explain to the colonel that he would see the Fjords on his way to 60°N. He was upset a little as he wasn't flying – but I organised 40 hotel rooms in advance so a good 2 day R & R was enjoyed by all the detachment

After leaving the airforce and recoat air cargo it was 1982 so I went looking for employment. I went for an interview and a medical in London and was offered a job in Saudi-Arabia I was to be a hydrauic engineer on hawk missiles. I was part of a team replacing 20 Americans who because of tax reasons had to go home to America. Our job was to completely renew any unserviceale parts or values that had been in Saudi-Arabia for 4 years and occasionally washed down in sea-water so parts were corroded. All parts were sand-blasted and each item checked while I was thre (6 months) the 2 battery's I worked on were tested and both had direct hits – so I was quite pleased as I enjoyed the job aso the money I earnt.

When I returned home I met an old Raf Sgt who worked at Lynehamas a movements controlled who told me about a NE squadron being formed at Briz-Worton. A new movements squadron and he arranged for me to be interviewed by a Sq/Ldr who just happened to be his old boss.

I accepted the job (although I dropped down 1 position in rank) and I started the next week in ops it was an Auxiliary Raf Squadron (4624 Sqdn)??? ecting females to hump and dump 250lb boxes on a??? would be a touch to much. Plus extra money had to be spent for building female toilets etc but the air force started recruiting females, Im not sure now that the females ar still recruted but I??? suspect it will have died a natural death.

Because I had travelled most of the??? that auxiliary airmen would go to I had to write a precis about the bases facilities.

In 1985 I was replaced in operations and went back to instructing the recruits. All our recruits had to spend 14 days per year on a detachment. Sometimes Salisbury plain, camping out and using a field kitchen, tent erecting and all other drill movements. As there are 3 ways of instructing – 1 in a classroom – 2 in a hangar on wooden A/C, 3 on a real live A/C I was in charge of the live A/C type of instructing this meant that when 6 airmen went on their 14 days I had to accompany them. This may soon a little guiding them on the right paths but the detachmen overseas – Cyprus – Germany – Ascension Island they had to be shown the bases – accommodation – working area and supervised at all they did. So when 6 airmen went to Germany I went too and stayed for 6 weeks with the second and third & detachments. This also applied to the detachments at Cyprus and Acension Island. As more than 3 A/C types were used the recruits did well and received good reports from the movement officer 1/c their sections. At this time someone decided that females should be recruited in the movements aux squadron – they could be trim clerks and passenger clerks

I served on 4624 Sqdn till 1989, 7 seven total 7 very good years.

In 1989 I went for an interview at Oxford University – Exeter College and was employed as the college head porter. It was a good job and I met many nice people. The job when I first started had nothing computerised, or electronic??? press a button and side the main gates & they open and allow you to drive a car into the back quad.

I switch my television on now to catch the morning news and an old college student is the man presenter – there are 2 sisters one is on BBC1 & one on BBC2 the Chakrabarti sisters Nagwa & Reeta – although Nagwa is now married. It is good to see how they have progressed

I have heard that a chap who was a flying off pilot has just been promoted to air vice marshal. My youngest daughter used to babysit

when his 2 daughters were young. I believe his daughters are 28 &
30 years old now. I do like to hear about old friends getting on well in
their careers. I have been informed that altogether some of the auxiliary
airmen I recruited an instructed have now 2 flt/lt, 2 sq/ldrs and 1 wing
commander all still in the Raf auxiliary air force. (4624 sqn)

In 1999 I retired from my job at Oxford University. And in 2002
moved to live in Spain – 5 miles from Mabella. I must agree the
weather and temperatures suit me down to the ground.

I suppose I ought to describe my life as a journey from a
steel labourer then Raf (24 yrs) then world traveller then missile
mechanic, a mover into the auxiliary air force and soon to have
employment at Oxford University (for 10 years) then retirement. I
still travelled and moved to live in Spain for 5 years. My last move
was to a region of the north-east in the next village to my wife's
brother the move seems to have worked out ok, we are both happy
with the area and like the people we have met here. My sister lives
just 50 miles away and we have the seaside on our door step. Our
neighbors are??? because we are all over 55 years we all seem
to??? help each other. Most of my life now is spent backwards
& forwards either to my local doctor of the nearby hospitals. My
biggest problems now are weeding the flagstones in my small
garden, raking the marine pebbles on the other side of my garden.
The largest job to be done is to paint the garden shed once a year,
otherwise life is quite slow and I thank myself that I married my
good wife as she never seems to stop. God bless her.

T.G.

Since moving north my wife and I travelled 5 day to New York
on Queen Elizabeth the 2 years ago we visited my daughte and
my wifes sister who both live on Vancouver Island. So my days of
travelling are not quite over.

I still want to visit Russia, China & New Zealand although
last year I visited East Germany, Czechoslovakia, Teneria Reno &
Vancouver (Mainland). So after flying for 31 years & total 17,000
hrs, I still want to travel.

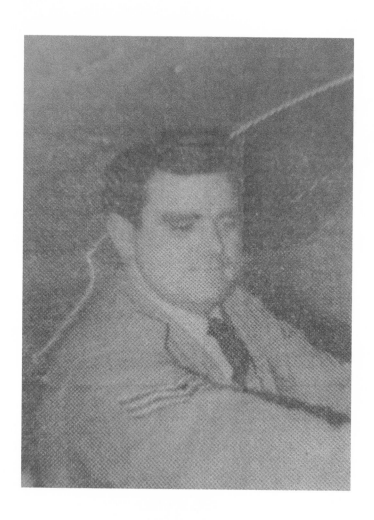

Lightning Source UK Ltd.
Milton Keynes UK
UKHW040725110220
358531UK00001B/95